Greenhouse Hygge

The House of My Growing Dreams

Lise-Lotte Loomer

◆ FriesenPress

Suite 300 – 990 Fort St
Victoria, BC, V8V 3K2
Canada

www.friesenpress.com

ISBN
978-1-4602-9301-0 (Hardcover)
978-1-4602-9302-7 (Paperback)
978-1-4602-9303-4 (eBook)

1. GARDENING GREENHOUSES

Distributed to the trade by The Ingram Book Company

Table of Contents

"'Hygge', pronounced "Heug gha". A Danish concept that doesn't have an English equivalent translation – the idea is of a cozy, warm atmosphere surrounded by people you love, family, friends, colleagues; but it can also be with people you don't know, with someone you meet and feel a connection. Hygge can be planned, but it can also happen spontaneously. Hygge also happens in solitude. It's an atmosphere, a feeling that captures life's essence.

Hygge is being present, authentic, content in the now, without thinking about it, it's just being...... in the moment. Hygge is a sanctuary for the soul".

—Anne Sture Tucker

This is the story of the greenhouse my mom gave me when she was in hospice, how we moved it into my garden, and how I made it my own.

My Story

When my mom first told me that she wanted me to have her greenhouse, I was extremely grateful. But the process of moving this frail, thirty-eight-year-old aluminum and glass house was not just physically daunting, it was also emotionally taxing.

When I take on a project, I need to feel the vision and purpose of what I'm creating. Thinking about the greenhouse project, I reflected on the life this little house had lived and the life it was about to transition into. My mom hadn't been inside the greenhouse in the past five years; a very gentle and caring gardener—who reported everything about the garden to my mom—cared for it in her place. Mom was in a wheelchair and faced health challenges that kept her out of her garden. She missed it. She knew where every plant in her garden was; she could visualize each one and ask about the plants that lived around it. The inhabitants of her garden were imprinted on her memory.

When my parents moved to a new lot, Mom moved all the plants up the street in a wheelbarrow. She built that garden from scratch plant by plant, acquiring other plants along the way so that after forty-six years, she had created an enchanting secret oasis on a city lot. My parents moved the house up the street too, but that's a story for another day.

Now firmly rooted in my garden, the little glass house carries with it so many memories of my mom: how happy she was pottering about, propagating roses, and starting seedlings while listening to a little radio that ran on a small battery, the antenna positioned just right so she could listen to classical music. Her favourite composer was Chopin. She would often have her tea out there, and if you came out to chat, she would generously open a small weathered tin to share a little licorice—the Danes love their licorice and their chocolate.

inhospitable. Of course the greenhouse provided protection from the rain showers in the spring, but it also offered refuge from the noise of the neighbours and the traffic. Inside the glass walls there was a feeling of safety for the plants and for the gardener. Inside, this place radiated—mostly to be appreciated by gardeners—with the hope of life and the awe of new growth. The excitement to find a seed pushing the soil away, the subtle changes in the number of leaves a little plant put out, the buds slowly opening, and the scent of the orange blossom that Mom was babysitting for me because it didn't like living in my Vancouver apartment: this was her greenhouse. It sat there for thirty-eight years, and now it was going to move to my garden. I only live an eight minute drive away, but I felt like I was moving the greenhouse to a different world. When I thought about moving the greenhouse, I wanted to create that same feeling: I wanted to create a haven to celebrate and appreciate the wonders of life, the feeling of peace and the calm that comes with being in nature. I wanted to incorporate the Danish concept of hygge.

Mom's greenhouse had the sense of being outside—outside in the fresh air, outside of the house—and so you felt away (in those days) from the phone and from the mundane inside tasks, and outside of the obligations imposed by long to-do lists. But her greenhouse also had elements of being inside. It was located only metres from the ocean where the wind would whistle up the street and make the greenhouse a safe haven for when the secluded garden on a city lot seemed

Lise-Lotte's Hygge

When Mom gave me her greenhouse, I knew that I needed a clear vision and a list of goals in order to install it with purpose in my own garden. The greenhouse held such a special place in my mom's life; I wanted to create an environment just as cozy as the one she had built. So I wrote a list of what the greenhouse would need to encompass. Here is what I wrote down:

- My greenhouse is going to have all the elements that made it special for my mom. But I recognize that it will be different because I'm different from her—I'm more social.

- I want my friends to feel welcome, so my greenhouse has to have room to sit and enjoy a cup of tea and have something delicious to eat. We'll need a space where we can sit inside and enjoy a conversation in the relative privacy that a small glass house provides, breathing in the beautiful scent of whatever's in season: lily-of-the-valley, hyacinths, or wall flowers.

- Finding a place to be still and quiet in the everyday is important to me. Practising mindfulness and noticing the small changes in my seedlings provides a sense of wonder that is both reminiscent of my childhood and attributed to the wisdom of age. I intend to practice gratitude for the peace that I live in. The greenhouse will need to have a comfortable chair for me to sit and drink tea or enjoy a glass of wine. It will be a place to think and to dream about what to plant next, both in my garden and in my life.

❧ *Here is the greenhouse in Mom's garden with my daughter Ilse and her friend Katherine*

• I host a lot of celebrations with family and friends. There are soccer balls, ping pong balls, croquet balls, and basketballs flying around my back garden, so my little house has to find a place where it can "weather" the action.

- I want my greenhouse to be a focal point in the garden. After all, the glass means that the plants inside are visually as much a part of the garden as the ones that already have a home outside.

- There's something quite elegant about the iconic structure of a little house, so clever in its simple construction. It is the generator of seedlings that supply the garden for the summer season. It will protect the little plants until the weather warms up enough for them to live in the big outside world. It will also allow me to have plants that would not otherwise grow in my area, such as orange trees.

- The greenhouse will extend the seasons and my days in the garden because I will be able to sit out there in any kind of weather and late into the evening. My little glass house will provide shelter, protecting me and my plants from the elements while still allowing me to be outside.

photograph by Ilse Loomer-Scott

I knew this was a great deal to expect from a little house that only measures six by eight feet. Could this little structure really be a cozy space that appeals to the olfactory senses, a calm and quiet place to practice meditation, a backdrop for garden celebrations, a focal point tucked into the perennial bed under the white lilac, *and* a shelter that protects both the plants and the gardener? Could this little place really do all that?

I hope you will take inspiration from my experiences and give yourself a moment to make a good cup of your favourite tea, sit in a comfortable chair in your garden, connect with some inspiration, and create a dream of your own special greenhouse that could be the centrepiece of your garden and the foundation of your garden life.

May *Greenhouse Hygge* inspire you to create the house of *your* growing dreams!

Happy dreaming. Happy being.

Lise-Lotte

Moving a Glass House

My dad gave the greenhouse to my mom as a gift. While Mom was usually the practical one in our family, Dad was the one who put it together. Twice. He realized that he put it together inside out the first time when he went to put in the glass panels. So I knew that this "kit" from New Zealand, purchased from Woodward's all those years ago in a series of boxes, was like a puzzle.

Over the course of three weekends, working into the dark and cold of February, my patient life partner Tereus and I packed each of the remaining glass panels (there were a few missing: one due to an errant soccer ball and who knows what happened to the others). Before wrapping them in newsprint, we cleaned each one with wet newsprint and rags to remove the accumulation of moss and sea salt.

One morning while the children were in school, my dear friend Erika came with her truck and her practicality muscle ("let's use our iPhones to record every step as we take this apart") and

Photograph by Erika Herrmann

together we disassembled and carried the sides of the greenhouse onto her truck. We left the glass in the small end pieces, placed old foam mattresses between the panels, and drove *very* slowly, taking the long way home.

Before Erika helped me move the greenhouse, I had started digging in our backyard. I found out quickly that there were huge rocks under the surface of our little piece of property. Tereus applied some ingenuitive thinking and moved the rocks using levers. I dug two feet down and our golden retriever Daisy and I moved first sand and then small stones by wheelbarrow from the front driveway to the backyard. Daisy met me at the side gate and followed me to the backyard as I dumped load after load of sand and rocks. After a while, she resorted to sitting in the grass and raising an eyebrow to make sure there was no change to the program. As with many people, our knowledge of how to lay bricks so they're flat and don't wobble (who would have thought that something so heavy lying on a soft surface like sand and small gravel could wobble?) came from watching YouTube videos. The picture you see is of Daisy "helping" me level the site. With my iPhone, I recorded the progress of the project and shared the excitement with Mom when I visited

her once or twice a day in hospice. I know she was thrilled that my dad's gift to her would live on, but more than that, that it would be a space to enjoy and appreciate the garden and share our love of plants.

If in gardening the most important part is to prepare healthy soil, so in building the most important part is to prepare a solid foundation. I think the same can be said for relationships and learning. A solid foundation provides a stable base on which everything can be subsequently built. Because I decided that this little house needed to be as hospitable to people as it was to plants, we raised it slightly by placing the sides of the house on beams. This meant that when it came time to place Mom's handmade cedar shelves inside, we were off by a few centimetres. Mom had built the shelves to make use of each centimetre and they fit perfectly. Luckily, Tereus was able to shave off a little length to make them fit. I thought at

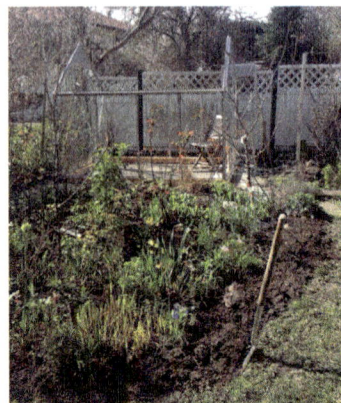

the time that one day I might update the interior of the greenhouse, but since I love the patina of old wood and since Mom made them, I opted to leave them in. Having lived with them for a couple of years now in their current home, I have no desire to replace them. They were well thought out and they work so well for my height, which is the same as Mom's was.

Despite all the measuring and the weight of the beams, once we got the greenhouse up, there was still a small space where little things could get in. So between the beam and the cement square, Tereus sprayed an expandable sealing form. Once it dried, we cut off the extra and covered it on the inside with a small length of wood. When it was in my mom's garden, she had glass jars tucked in the inside walls to keep out the animals that got in and ate her spring bulbs. Mom was always very innovative when it came to using everyday objects to solve problems so that she didn't have to go to the store. But Mom's greenhouse sat directly on the ground in her garden, and even with gravel inside, the mice—and presumably the rats—got in and ate what they wanted.

Moving Into a Glass House

In my research of how other people have used their greenhouses, I've noticed that many people have set up a separate place to do their planting. But in my garden, I don't have a separate place, so I do my planting, transplanting and flower arranging on the counter in my greenhouse. Also, much of my planting takes place in the early spring when the weather can be quite cool, so I prefer to stand out of the wind to plant seeds, transplant seedlings, or plant the cuttings of roses.

In my attempt to keep the space as free from unnecessary clutter as possible, I have only used two colours: blue and terracotta. I want the plants to be the stars. The one exception is the chartreuse linen cushion I made. I love natural materials and I've tried to have as little plastic in the greenhouse as possible, apart from the plant pots. Later in the summer, when most plants have moved into the ground in the surrounding garden, I have only basil, my orange tree, and tomatoes growing inside.

The faded white fence, with its unattractive lattice design, was a bit of a problem because to make way for the greenhouse, I removed many of the plants that had hidden it before. Given the time of year (it was too early to paint), I found an alternative in a willow panel that gave me a dark surface with some texture and provided some privacy as well. I understand that it's a temporary solution tied to the existing fence, but it's worked well for the past two years.

I wanted to have a little patio in front of the greenhouse where I could have a few containers with scented annuals and perhaps some roses. I also wanted a place where I could sit with a friend during the summer when it's too hot to be inside. But I didn't realize that we hadn't accounted for that in our measurements. So Daisy and I started digging again. She does her digging in short bursts of energy when her human takes a break for tea, but every little bit helps when you have to loosen the soil. A pickaxe for the hardpan doesn't hurt either when the hole is a little deeper. As you can see in the photographs, we have left it with just some small gravel. One day, I will add more cement slabs and make it more finished.

My mom's brother gave us two blackcurrant bushes that provided a cozy barrier from the raspberry patch and the gate beyond, but that also limited the space we had for a patio. At the moment, I have room only for one chair, which sits out there in the summer to make more room for the tomato planters that sit on the floor inside the greenhouse. If there's rain and I want to sit inside, I just move it in. In the cooler weather, the chair comes inside.

Considering the Site

I wanted a sunny place, but not one with full day sun. I placed my greenhouse where it is because the huge poplar means it has early morning sun and the lilac provides slight shade in the late afternoon. The greenhouse is also placed where I can see it from the kitchen window and from my covered deck, where we eat most of our meals in the late spring, summer, and even into the warmer days of fall. I love looking down into the garden when it's cold and dark outside and seeing the solar lights that create a cozy presence while I do the dishes and dream about what's growing.

I wanted the greenhouse to be part of the action so that when we throw parties, it could be a helpful spot to place drinks in ice buckets and place appetizers up on the top shelf. During celebrations, friends often comment on the peace they find as they step into the greenhouse to pour a glass of wine or a cup of tea. It's a way of giving permission to go into this rather small space. I also wanted a place to sit where I could enjoy the long view of my perennial bed. The greenhouse has become such a lovely private space to meditate. Practically speaking, this particular site also meant taking out or moving the fewest and easiest-to-move plants.

If you're considering building a greenhouse in your backyard, there are a few things you might wish to think about when it comes to its location in your garden:

- How many and what type of plants do you need to move in order to create space?
- Do you want to see your greenhouse from inside your house?
- Are there any municipality requirements about how close to the fence your greenhouse can be?
- Is the site flat?
- Where is the sun in different seasons?

- Have you considered your neighbours? Can you protect the glass if there are children who play with balls?
- What is the drainage like?
- When sitting inside, what do you want to look out at?
- Will there be large roots to remove when you dig out the space for the greenhouse?
- Have you considered the natural light?

In Victoria, our growing seasons are often slightly ahead of other places, given our mild winters. The natural light in my garden influences my greenhouse in a big way, which you can see in the following photos.

Very early morning sun

Early morning sun

Midday in the summer

Midday in the early summer

Evening sun

Later in the day

I use clothes pins to hang my garden gloves for three reasons: I can find them again, they are dry for the next use and no little bugs climb into the finger tips to surprise me next time I wear them.

There are many tools that you will need for a functioning greenhouse. I've compiled a list of essentials to get you started.

On the practical side:

- Markers for seeds
- Clothes pins
- Jute string/twine and scissors
- Scissors for herbs
- Potting soil
- Organic fertilizer
- A small shovel
- A watering can with small holes in the sprinkler spout to gently water seedlings
- A small thermometer
- A small broom
- Cotton cloth
- Cloth for washing the windows
- Hooks
- Pots
- Shelving

On the wish list:

- Soil blocker or block maker
- A wooden newspaper pot maker
- A tray for the pots to sit in and catch the water

On the cozy side:

- A small speaker to plug an iPhone into to listen to music
- Solar lights
- Licorice
- Good quality chocolate (on cool days, otherwise it melts)
- Candles and matches in a tin
- Automatic outdoor candles for the off season when there isn't enough sunlight to charge the solar lights
- A comfortable chair and pillow
- A small side table

Mom's Advice

Sitting in a sunny window in Mom's hospital room, I sat close to her in the only chair while she sat in her wheelchair, and with tears in my eyes, asked her how I could live in this world without her. At that point, we knew she was terminally ill, but she hadn't been moved into hospice yet. Over the years I had always been able to talk to her about anything. During those times when parenting was really hard, when it was lonely and exhausting, I could call her and she would encourage me. Sitting across from me in her hospital room that day, she looked over at me reassuringly and said in her beautiful, soft, strong voice, "Nature will take care of you." And it has. In the days, weeks, and years that have followed, being in the garden with her plants, with her roses or clematis, is what's kept me at peace. Walking Daisy on the beach and seeing the seaweed that's swept up on the beach in the fall, I always remember the times when I would go with my mom to a small cove and collect the heavy seaweed into bags and drag them to the orange Volkswagen van to get it all home to her garden and spread it over her perennial and vegetable beds to amend the soil. These are the times when I feel grounded.

It is in nature, whether in its somewhat contrived domestic form or in its wild essence, where I feel most at peace. No matter what problem I need to solve, I step out into my garden, don my blue gardening gloves (or not), and get my hands busy with the tasks that my garden needs me to do: pruning, pulling weeds, digging, and pulling away bugs. These tasks keep my conscious mind busy enough that my unconscious mind can get on with the real work of solving the problem at hand, settling my emotions, or moving to being more centred.

Observations

After living with my dream greenhouse for the past two years, I can now say that it has been a wonderful addition to my garden and to my sense of self. Over the last twenty-five years, I have gardened in everything from extensive container gardens, to an allotment garden, to patio gardens, and finally to my own garden where everything is planted in the ground. Having lived with my greenhouse for two years now, here are some tips I have learned from our time together:

- Your greenhouse will feel and look shorter as the plants grow up around it.

- When you plan out the shelves in your greenhouse, keep in mind that when you water your plants, water will drip through to the next shelf down, so don't put anything underneath that could be damaged (or use trays).

- Move the pots around regularly so you can see any bugs or slugs and remove them.

- Completely seal the bottom of greenhouse so nothing can sneak in and eat bulbs and seeds.

- Don't place anything on the lower shelves that your puppy or other animals could get into, not even fertilizer, organic matter, or root starter.

- Be mindful of the colours you choose: I chose terracotta/glass and blue. Otherwise, the small space can look too cluttered.

Your greenhouse can be many things. Mine is…

- a cozy sight at the bottom of my garden under the lilac tree
- a place to try new seeds that I've never grown before
- a place to grow tomatoes and basil in a lovely warm spot
- a place to sit after school with my daughters and hear about their school days
- a bar for drinks in the evening
- a sideboard for appetizers that Daisy can't reach
- a place for conversations
- a place to be silent and still in all weather conditions at all times of year

🌱 *My girls have given me some very thoughtful garden gifts over the years. Here are two examples, one that uses a line of a poem that we had to memorize as children and another that says, "Mom's Garden you can write the name of the plant here." It's a sticker made with chalkboard paint.*

Celebrations in the garden

🌱 *Outdoor movie night and birthday celebrations*

🌱 *Enjoying our meals outside with protection from the late day sun.*

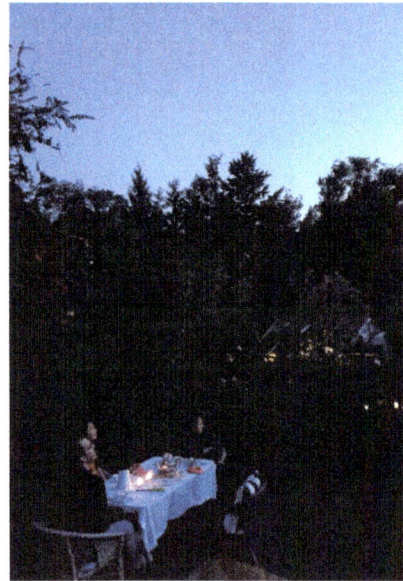

🌱 *"I think I see the first star!"*

Family gatherings with Nouria and Magnus. Thank you to the three Danish/Canadian children, Toran, Maja and Annika for coming to the party.

❧ *My dear friend Krista Hennebury made this pillow for me with Liberty fabric. I have fond memories of visiting the Liberty of London store on a couple of occasions by myself, long after Mom fell in love with their silky soft cottons. I have made lovely napkins from old Liberty dresses that Mom made for herself, attaching a small piece of linen to the back—a very useful project I learned from Krista.*

Recipes

As a tribute to everything my mom has taught me, I'd like to share two of her favourite recipes. I hope you will share these recipes with the members of your family and enjoy them for years to come.

MOM'S MARZIPAN CHOCOLATE TORTE

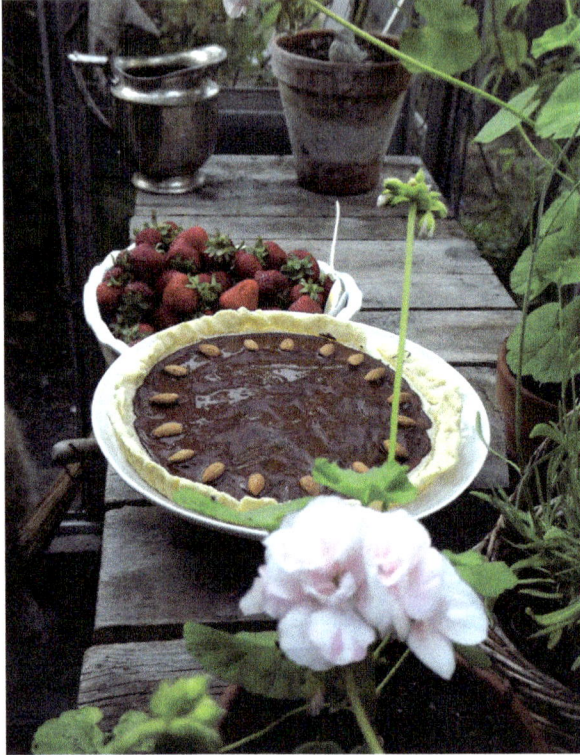

For the crust:

- ½ cup butter
- ¼ cup sugar
- 1 egg yolk
- 1 ¼ cup flour

Cream together the butter, sugar, and egg yolk. Mix in the flour. Wrap the dough in plastic wrap and let it rest in the fridge for at least two hours. Once the dough is chilled, press it into your tart dish. Keep cool until baking time.

For the filling:

- ½ cup sifted icing sugar
- ⅓ cup almond paste
- 2 egg whites

Soften almond paste in the microwave. Add egg whites and icing sugar. Beat until it forms a thick liquid. Pour the filling into the unbaked crust. Bake at 325 degrees for approximately twenty minutes, or until the torte is golden brown and solid in the middle. Scatter chocolate pieces on top of the torte while it's still hot from the oven. The heat will melt the chocolate and you can then spread it around in a thin layer. Add whole almonds to decorate if you wish.

MOM'S ALL-PURPOSE COOKIES

- 1 cup plus 1 tablespoon butter
- ½ cup sugar
- 2 eggs
- 3 ½ cups flour

Beat together the butter and sugar. Add eggs and beat until combined. Add flour and mix. Shape dough into a disk, wrap in plastic, and refrigerate for at least half an hour. When it's chilled, roll out the dough and cut with cookie cutters. Bake at 350 degrees until cookies are light brown. Decorate cooled cookies with icing (icing sugar, a little water, and colouring paste or a drop or two of food colouring).

Ripples

My greenhouse and my garden provide a place for me to live as close to the rhythm of nature as possible. Apart from the new beams, sand, and gravel, we moved this greenhouse and rebuilt it using almost everything we already had, including the patio tiles from another part of the garden. Mom would have loved how we didn't need to visit the store and were able to be creative and re-purpose items in order to appreciate what we had already in a new way. After all, the benches she made were built with wood she gathered at the beach.

In a world where we all need to look for ways to take care of our planet, here are a few ways that I make small contributions every day.

In the spring:
I have mason bees and I plant flowers that attract bees and feed hummingbirds. I often place dryer lint outside for the birds to use in their nest building. In my greenhouse, I start seeds for friends as a way of sharing a seed pack. I collect seeds to plant next year. I buy from local or regional seed companies, who also have the most pertinent growing information for my area. When my girls were little, we planted a garden together and they had their own space to grow the seeds they chose at the nursery. They experienced the thrill of peeking under the leaves to see if the strawberries were "ready yet" and the mystery and excitement of where the potatoes were "hiding" in the ground as they went out with a bowl and "tickled the potatoes," as their "Mormor" would say (Mormor is "mother's mother" in Danish). I leave watering cans outside the greenhouse with their lids off to catch any rainwater. Soon I will install water barrels to catch and store the rainwater from the roof.

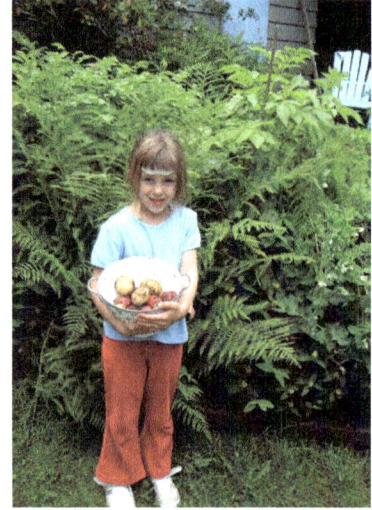

🌱 *Our friends helping in the children's area of our garden in North Vancouver: Abby, Holden and Max Korbin*

In the summer:
I give flowers that I have grown to my friends instead of buying flowers that have travelled great distances.

I collect water (from leftover tea or sport bottles) in the kitchen in a jug and water my plants with it. As my girls have grown, I've taken them to farmers' markets and bought them fresh fruits and veggies for them to munch on right there.

I've taken my international students berry picking and to farmer's markets to experience what real strawberries and raspberries taste like. Many of these students had never had fresh fruit and couldn't get over the how sweet it is.

I don't use any pesticides. I mulch.

In the fall:
I leave flowers to go to seed so the birds have something to eat through the winter.

Conclusion

The greenhouse and I have put down roots in the now.

Sitting in my greenhouse after two years together, things look different—both for obvious reasons and for more subtle ones.

Obviously, the plants have filled in and I have to be judicious with my pruning so that I still have a view and don't feel as though the garden is taking over.

Things look different because they are different. I have moved through the various stages of grief and I've come to a place of appreciation for the experience of my mom's last days. I can appreciate her last years and find more balance with remembering the fun times and the difficult ones. I live with great gratitude for the experience of being her daughter and will draw on her skills and wisdom as I raise my own daughters and the ones living in our home from other countries. I still haven't mastered the art of propagating roses as my mom did, so clearly there's still work to be done.

With time, my perspective has changed. When I first started writing this book, I imagined the greenhouse as my mother's space. But I'm a planner by nature; I'm always thinking one step ahead. There's a piece of that equation that serves me well when thinking about which seeds or bulbs need to be planted where and when so they'll happily bloom and produce months from now. As I live with the greenhouse now, I've realized that it's a gift and a daily reminder to be living in the present. The scents of the flowers, of the herbs, and of the tomatoes instantly bring me into the present moment. The knowledge that the roses will only look like that today and that tomorrow there will be slight changes keeps me firmly grounded in the now. The feeling of the warm sun shifting when the sun goes behind a cloud, the sound of the soft rain starting and then reaching a crescendo as it pelts down on the glass above my head; these small moments bring me peace. If one has time to sit a little longer, the birds will start to sing again. Being present to enjoy and appreciate these minute changes keeps me—literally—grounded. My greenhouse has put down roots, and so have I.

Epilogue

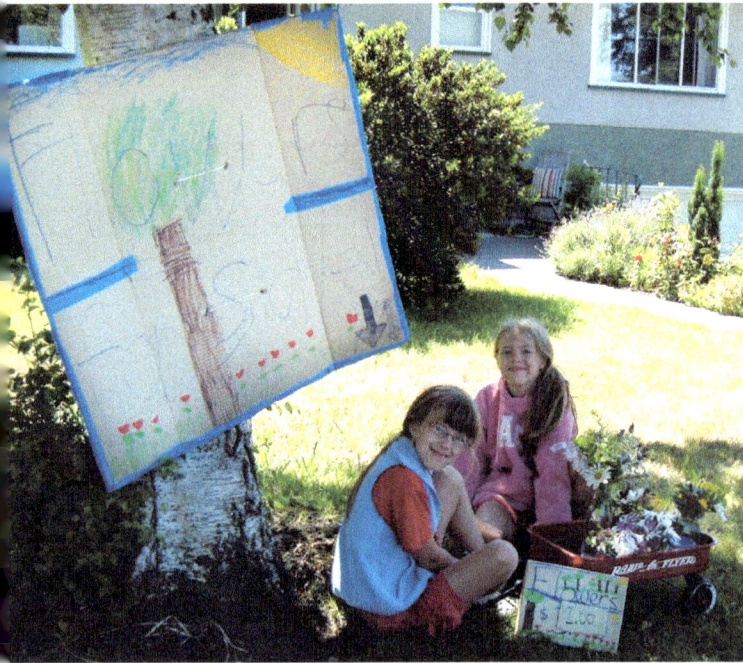

Currently, our wonderful daughters and I are starting an urban flower farm to supplement the girls' summer income for university. This is our first year. We have removed our front lawn; moved a large California lilac, a rhododendron, and some other cedar shrubs; built raised beds; filled them with a good soil mix; and put up deer netting. Although we're right in the middle of an urban setting, we see a great many deer munching their way through our garden city. I'm starting some seeds (like sweet peas) in my greenhouse as a way of extending the season.

Partygreen flowers will provide our customers with wonderful bouquets delivered to their friends and family to say: I'm here for you, I'm celebrating you, or I appreciate you.

As a child, I watched and helped my mom, who was a very generous and lovely gardener. With Mom's permission, my sister and I used to pick her flowers and sell them at a stand on the street outside our home, as we would also do

with lemonade. We didn't have any customers, so Mom would come along and cheerfully buy back her own flowers and arrange them in a vase for the dinner table. She would even share with Dad where she had purchased those lovely flowers! Moms are the best sports.

This new venture is a huge leap of faith, given that my only flower-buying customer to date has been my mom, and she isn't here to buy my flowers anymore. Come to think of it, she even came along when the girls were little and bought my flowers from them when they set up shop in a little red wagon out on our boulevard. Mormors are great sports too!

🌱 *This rose, which now grows in my garden is taken from a plant that was in Mom's garden grown from a cutting from Mom's Canadian mom, Mrs. Margaret Denny. The vase is a gift from my friend Laura Wanamaker. Madam Blue – the 1930's Danish enamel coffee pot looks lovely with flowers. Mom hand painted the board in the background for our playhouse in her garden. Dad built the playhouse from wood collected at the beach and it still stands forty eight years later for the new owner's family.*

Acknowledgements

I didn't achieve my greenhouse dreams and subsequent book on my own. I am grateful to Tereus Scott, my life partner, and to our fabulous daughters, Chloe Elisabeth and Ilse May Loomer-Scott.

I must also give a special mention to my puppy dog, Daisy, who has been my constant companion for the past eight years and whom my mom loved so much. She is the best gardening/quilting/knitting/cooking/baking/writing/meditating dog a gal ever had. She's also a very good listener.

I appreciate my sister and fellow garden lover, Anne-Lise Loomer, and her husband Darren Douglas, whose beautiful children Nouria and Magnus have used the greenhouse as a BC Ferry and sailed away—"All aboard, Auntie!"

I appreciate Erika Herrmann for both her physical and emotional strength in the process of moving the greenhouse.

Thank you to Anne Sture Tucker for the idea to write this book in the first place, for listening, for your friendship, your patience, and the skills you provided for me to mirror when I was achieving hygge.

To the gardener who lovingly and respectfully looked after Mom's garden for the last five years, known to our family as Kasha: Thank you.

I appreciate my friends for helping me with their encouragement, suggestions, and ideas. I am strong because of the special people around me, who, among all of their other attributes, are positive, supportive, and honest, and who lovingly helped me during this transition: Rosemary Barlow, Julie Bedell, Deborah Block, Elizabeth Brennan, Joan Carruthers, Jiyeon Chung, Heather Dewey, Gillian Donald, Jan Drent, Janet Gear, Katarina Harms, Krista Harris, Krista Hennebury, Lindiann Hopkins, Arlene Konut, Henrietta Langran, Carmen Lassooij, Elizabeth Louchran, Diana Life, Sarah McLeod, Judy MacKinnon, Mary Anne Marchildon, Lenora Moore, Tamara Navaratnam, Vicky Nielsen, Leslie Norwood, Christina Nyers, Chrystal Palaty, Tia Primrose, the late Bruce Scott, Wendy Scott, Kim Sheppard, Alison Shillington, Carolyn Taylor, Karen Thompson, Laura Wanamaker, Jackie Wheaton, and Del Whelan.

I have grown in my understanding of the plants I choose to surround myself with. I have grown as a daughter, a mother, a partner, a sister, and as an individual with lovely friends in her life. For all of this, I am eternally grateful.

This book is a tribute to my mom for her love of gardening, her appreciation of nature, and her sense of awe in the natural world, which by observation I have learned. It's also a tribute to my father, who gave her the gift of a greenhouse in the first place and always supported her love of gardening by giving her as birthday gifts beautifully mature mushroom manure and fine French perfume – Chanel no. 5.

When I open a good quality dark chocolate bar in the greenhouse with my family for tea, I can hear my mother's voice saying, "I have chocolate…shall we be friends?"

Elisabeth Loomer (nee Baess) April 2, 1930 to April 9, 2013

photograph by Chloe Loomer-Scott

Lise-Lotte Loomer is a facilitator living in Victoria BC with her family, international students and her constant companion, Daisy, their golden retriever.

Lise-Lotte's blog is partygreen.ca where she shares many ways to create hygge in your garden and in your life.

Lise-Lotte loves nothing more than to spend time in her garden enjoying the scent of mock orange and roses, listening to the birds singing, and watching the hummingbird visit the flowers. She appreciates spending time with family and friends in her garden and harvesting strawberries and raspberries on the way to sit down to share stories over Earl Grey tea with a homemade treat. Lise-Lotte celebrates the ordinary, the timeless and the simple with gratitude.

CPSIA information can be obtained
at www.ICGtesting.com
Printed in the USA
LVOW05s0006011216
515210LV00009B/11/P